My First Poem

North London

Edited By Donna Samworth

First published in Great Britain in 2017 by:

Young Writers

Young Writers
Coltsfoot Drive
Peterborough
PE2 9BF
Telephone: 01733 890066
Website: www.youngwriters.co.uk

All Rights Reserved
Book Design by Ashley Janson
© Copyright Contributors 2017
SB ISBN 978-1-78820-128-5
Printed and bound in the UK by BookPrintingUK
Website: www.bookprintinguk.com
YB0320CZ

Foreword

Young Writers was established in 1991 with the aim of encouraging writing skills in young people and giving them the opportunity to see their work in print. Poetry is a wonderful way to introduce young children to the idea of rhyme and rhythm and helps learning and development of communication, language and literacy skills.
'My First Poem' was created to introduce nursery and preschool children to this wonderful world of poetry. They were given a template to fill in with their own words, creating a poem that was all about them.
We are proud to present the resulting collection of personal and touching poems in this anthology, which can be treasured for years to come.

Jenni Bannister

Editorial Manager

Contents

Fountain Montessori Preschool, Edgware

Gabriel Hammond Rodriguez (4)	1
Tobi Jordan Jide-Ajagbe (4)	2
Anay Swapnil Ruparella (4)	3
Tarangini Ladva (4)	4
Vedant Dev Solanki (4)	5
Dhilan Surendran (3)	6
Naviana Ashok Gorasia (3)	7
Nikil Muthiah (3)	8
Kimorah Edwards-Annan (4)	9
Anaiya Mehta (3)	10
Sam Jalil (3)	11
Arianna Mahal (3)	12
Avneet Batti (3)	13
Kailen Vaghjiani (4)	14
Aaryan Tailor (4)	15
Mia Vaghjiani (3)	16
Ersi Aliu (3)	17
Lara Gagneja (4)	18
Darah Uloroh (4)	19
Daniel Rafael Lavric (3)	20
Sarah Cherifi (4)	21
Ria Vaghjiani (4)	22

Kidz Kabin @ Fortismere, London

Shakiel Qayyum (3)	23
Alexandros McDermott (4)	24
Peggy Kaye (4)	25
Mazzie Chambers (4)	26

Jaia Slade (4)	27
Tatiana Gurevich (4)	28
Hin Van Der Linden (3)	29

Kidz Kabin @ Pembroke Studios, London

Oliver Balsiger (4)	30
Wojciech Karwecki (4)	31
Noah Bardsley (4)	32
George Coulson (4)	33
Niamh Bird (4)	34
Huey Beck (4)	35
Oliver Birdsey (3)	36
Ioav Baldwin (4)	37
Darshan Iyngkaran (4)	38
Vian Matovu (3)	39
Liam Edwards (3)	40
Vernel Matovu (3)	41
Kaan Erdem (4)	42
Ruby Ayetigbo-Bamgbose (4)	43
Elai Ben Ari (4)	44
Amiya Fakey (3)	45
Violet Foran (3)	46
Daria Sgnaolin (4)	47
Kianna George (4)	48
Zara Beresford (4)	49
Maggie McLean (4)	50
Mia Scarso Borioli (3)	51
Oscar Du Rose (3)	52
Erin Henson (3)	53
George Love (3)	54
Freya Erdem (4)	55

Little Angels Schoolhouse, London

Jacob Corrigan (3)	56
Jahmal Aston Walker-Stewart (2)	57
Hector (3)	58
Olamide Bickersteth (4)	59
Rufus Edwin Finch (3)	60
Aiden Kyle Samuel-Maraj (4)	61
Arman Chajai (3)	62
Asher Brew (3)	63
Iris Zacharladis (3)	64
Alivia Dovies-Mozo (3)	65
Merryn Ash (3)	66

Longfield Primary School, Harrow

Ishaani Mistry (4)	67
Bohanegan Senthil (4)	68
Maryam Mafaz (4)	69
Khushi Rashmi Darbar (4)	70
Alisha Mehta (4)	71
Maria Saya (3)	72
Haviya Arasenthan (4)	73
Krishan Prem Badhwar (4)	74
Ziya J Patel (4)	75
Ram Anand Kesar (3)	76
Aarusan Mathiyalagkan (4)	77
Vihara Pakalapati (4)	78
Maizie Grundy (4)	79
Lily Gutteridge (4)	80
Lojith Kirishanth (4)	81
Kannisha Sobinarth (4)	82
Chenaya Rajapaksha (4)	83
Anaya Bela Patel (3)	84
Jasmin Sehdev (4)	85
Thasvin Vijayatharan (4)	86
Kian Borkhataria (4)	87
Kian Wong (3)	88

Platform One Nursery, London

Adam David Humphreys (4)	89
Eliz Sevin Sarak (3)	90
Lara Cristina Coles (3)	91
Sam Bedworth (3)	92

Puddleducks Nursery, London

Eva Bauzaite (4)	93
Benicio Laurnagaray (3)	94

Raynham Primary School - Edmonton Nursery, London

Abiyah Adebayo (4)	95
Angelica Nyang (4)	96
Janelle Ajayi-Gabriel (4)	97
Zander Basson (4)	98
Prince Owusu Appiah Opokuware (3)	99
Eyasu Tesfaldet (4)	100
Dion Restelica (3)	101
Bonnie Edwards (3)	102
Khalia Archer (3)	103
Charlie Savva (4)	104
Mahdi Muhamed (4)	105
Stefania Elisa Craciun (4)	106
Cianna Pearce (4)	107
Lucca Christos Asaad-Morcos (3)	108
Berat Ergun (4)	109
Mari Smith-Addis (4)	110
Ojoma Onoji (3)	111

Scribbles Nursery, London

George Simpson (4)	112
Jennifer Kane (3)	113
Alexander Quinto (4)	114

Josephine Orczyk (4)	115
Vivienne O'Shea (3)	116
Sebastian Haward (3)	117
Damon Inwards (3)	118
Abigail Ross (3)	119
Lyra Price (3)	120
Saffron Hardyman (3)	121
Tuula Price (3)	122
Isa Davis (4)	123
Ariya Samra (3)	124
Sammy (3)	125
Henryk Baguet (3)	126
Emlyn Moxon (3)	127
Silver Emilia Hands Curry (3)	128
Daniel Savigni (3)	129
Aidan Hussain (3)	130
Jack Cohen (3)	131
Reyansh Siaharthan (3)	132

The Poems

Gabriel's First Poem

My name is Gabriel and I go to preschool,
My best friends are Darah and Vedent, who are really cool.
I watch everything on TV,
Playing animals and bouncy ball is lots of fun for me.
I just love spaghetti to eat,
And sometimes chocolate bars for a treat.
Blue is a colour I like a lot,
My bouncy ball is the best present I ever got.
My favourite people are Mummy and Daddy, who are gems,
So this, my first poem, is just for them!

Gabriel Hammond Rodriguez (4)
Fountain Montessori Preschool, Edgware

Tobi's First Poem

My name is Tobi and I go to preschool,
My best friends are Aaryan and Neo, who are really cool.
I watch Thomas the Tank Engine on TV,
Playing chess is lots of fun for me.
I just love pancakes to eat,
And sometimes marshmallows for a treat.
Blue is a colour I like a lot,
My Donald Duckness is the best present I ever got.
My favourite people are Mummy and Daddy,
who are gems,
So this, my first poem, is just for them!

Tobi Jordan Jide-Ajagbe (4)
Fountain Montessori Preschool, Edgware

Anay's First Poem

My name is **Anay** and I go to preschool,
My best friends are **Kailen and Gabi**, who are really cool.
I watch **PAW Patrol** on TV,
Playing **Magna-Tiles** is lots of fun for me.
I just love **pasta** to eat,
And sometimes **chocolate eggs** for a treat.
Blue and red are colours I like a lot,
My **crane** is the best present I ever got.
My favourite people are **Daddy and Mummy**, who are gems,
So this, my first poem, is just for them!

Anay Swapnil Ruparella (4)
Fountain Montessori Preschool, Edgware

Tarangini's First Poem

My name is Tarangini and I go to preschool,
My best friend is Anay, who is really cool.
I watch PAW Patrol on TV,
Playing Chase On The Case is lots of fun for me.
I just love Spaghetti to eat,
And sometimes chocolate for a treat.
Blue is a colour I like a lot,
My fire engine and yo-yo is the best present
I ever got.
My favourite people are Mummy, Daddy and family, who are gems,
So this, my first poem, is just for them!

Tarangini Ladva (4)
Fountain Montessori Preschool, Edgware

Vedant's First Poem

My name is **Vedant** and I go to preschool,
My best friends are **Darah and Daniel**, who are really cool.
I watch **PAW Patrol** on TV,
Playing **with my teddy** is lots of fun for me.
I just love **pasta** to eat,
And sometimes **chocolate** for a treat.
Pink is a colour I like a lot,
My **rocket** is the best present I ever got.
My favourite people are **Darah and Daniel**, who are gems,
So this, my first poem, is just for them!

Vedant Dev Solanki (4)
Fountain Montessori Preschool, Edgware

Dhilan's First Poem

My name is Dhilan and I go to preschool,
My best friends are Neo and Nikil, who are really cool.
I watch Peppa Pig on TV,
Playing with my cars is lots of fun for me.
I just love pasta to eat,
And sometimes cake for a treat.
Blue is a colour I like a lot,
My Lego crane is the best present I ever got.
My favourite people are Nanny and Grandad,
who are gems,
So this, my first poem, is just for them!

Dhilan Surendran (3)
Fountain Montessori Preschool, Edgware

Naviana's First Poem

My name is **Naviana** and I go to preschool,
My best friend is **Jyotimasi**, who is really cool.
I watch **Peppa Pig** on TV,
Playing **Lego** is lots of fun for me.
I just love **Weetabix** to eat,
And sometimes **cake** for a treat.
Pink and orange are colours I like a lot,
My **pink watch** is the best present I ever got.
My favourite people are **Mummy and Daddy**, who are gems,
So this, my first poem, is just for them!

Naviana Ashok Gorasia (3)
Fountain Montessori Preschool, Edgware

Nikil's First Poem

My name is Nikil and I go to preschool,
My best friend is Dhilan Surendran, who is really cool.
I watch Cars on TV,
Playing with racing cars is lots of fun for me.
I just love apples to eat,
And sometimes drumsticks for a treat.
Blue is a colour I like a lot,
My Blaze and the Monster Machine toy is the best present I ever got.
My favourite person is Daddy, who is a gem,
So this, my first poem, is just for them!

Nikil Muthiah (3)
Fountain Montessori Preschool, Edgware

Kimorah's First Poem

My name is **Kimorah** and I go to preschool,
My best friend is **Vedent**, who is really cool.
I watch **games** on TV,
Playing **with my teddies** is lots of fun for me.
I just love **rice and veggies** to eat,
And sometimes **choc cake** for a treat.
Pink is a colour I like a lot,
My **Mickey Mouse pillow** is the best present
I ever got.
My favourite person is **Tamara Miaia**, who is a gem,
So this, my first poem, is just for them!

Kimorah Edwards-Annan (4)
Fountain Montessori Preschool, Edgware

Anaiya's First Poem

My name is **Anaiya** and I go to preschool,
My best friend is **my sister Alysha**, who is really cool.
I watch **Frozen** on TV,
Playing **dolls** is lots of fun for me.
I just love **pasta and spaghetti** to eat,
And sometimes **chocolate** for a treat.
Pink and purple are colours I like a lot,
My **Lego** is the best present I ever got.
My favourite person is **Poppie**, who is a gem,
So this, my first poem, is just for them!

Anaiya Mehta (3)
Fountain Montessori Preschool, Edgware

Sam's First Poem

My name is Sam and I go to preschool,
My best friend is Neo, who is really cool.
I watch Power Rangers on TV,
Playing with lorries is lots of fun for me.
I just love pasta to eat,
And sometimes sweets for a treat.
Blue is a colour I like a lot,
My Spider-Man is the best present I ever got.
My favourite people are Mummy, Daddy and Brother, who are gems,
So this, my first poem, is just for them!

Sam Jalil (3)
Fountain Montessori Preschool, Edgware

Arianna's First Poem

My name is **Arianna** and I go to preschool,
My best friend is **Naviana**, who is really cool.
I watch **Dora and Friends: Into the City!** on TV,
Playing **with my sister** is lots of fun for me.
I just love **pasta** to eat,
And sometimes **a pear** for a treat.
Pink is a colour I like a lot,
My **dolly** is the best present I ever got.
My favourite person is **my sister**, who is a gem,
So this, my first poem, is just for them!

Arianna Mahal (3)
Fountain Montessori Preschool, Edgware

Avneet's First Poem

My name is **Avneet** and I go to preschool,
My best friend is **Naviana**, who is really cool.
I watch **Do You Know?** on TV,
Playing **with all my toys** is lots of fun for me.
I just love **pasta** to eat,
And sometimes **sweets** for a treat.
Blue and purple are colours I like a lot,
My **stuffy dog** is the best present I ever got.
My favourite person is **Barbie**, who is a gem,
So this, my first poem, is just for them!

Avneet Batti (3)
Fountain Montessori Preschool, Edgware

Kailen's First Poem

My name is **Kailen** and I go to preschool,
My best friend is **Dhilan Shah**, who is really cool.
I watch **racing cars and Spider-Man** on TV,
Playing **with teddies** is lots of fun for me.
I just love **pesto pasta** to eat,
And sometimes **crisps** for a treat.
Blue is a colour I like a lot,
My **tractor** is the best present I ever got.
My favourite person is **Anay**, who is a gem,
So this, my first poem, is just for them!

Kailen Vaghjiani (4)
Fountain Montessori Preschool, Edgware

Aaryan's First Poem

My name is **Aaryan** and I go to preschool,
My best friend is **Nikal**, who is really cool.
I watch **PAW Patrol** on TV,
Playing **Spider-Man** is lots of fun for me.
I just love **lasagne** to eat,
And sometimes **chocolate** for a treat.
Orange and blue are colours I like a lot,
My **PAW Patrol** is the best present I ever got.
My favourite person is **Daddy**, who is a gem,
So this, my first poem, is just for them!

Aaryan Tailor (4)
Fountain Montessori Preschool, Edgware

Mia's First Poem

My name is Mia and I go to preschool,
My best friend is Ria, who is really cool.
I watch Cinderella on TV,
Playing with my doggy is lots of fun for me.
I just love spaghetti Bolognese to eat,
And sometimes sweets for a treat.
Grey is a colour I like a lot,
My walking doggy is the best present I ever got.
My favourite person is Ria, who is a gem,
So this, my first poem, is just for them!

Mia Vaghjiani (3)
Fountain Montessori Preschool, Edgware

Ersi's First Poem

My name is **Ersi** and I go to preschool,
My best friend is **Charlie**, who is really cool.
I watch **PAW Patrol** on TV,
Playing **on the slide** is lots of fun for me.
I just love **apples** to eat,
And sometimes **chocolate** for a treat.
Blue is a colour I like a lot,
My **blue car** is the best present I ever got.
My favourite person is **Daddy**, who is a gem,
So this, my first poem, is just for them!

Ersi Aliu (3)
Fountain Montessori Preschool, Edgware

Lara's First Poem

My name is **Lara** and I go to preschool,
My best friend is **Darah**, who is really cool.
I watch **Frozen** on TV,
Playing **dressing up** is lots of fun for me.
I just love **chicken** to eat,
And sometimes **hot chocolate** for a treat.
Pink is a colour I like a lot,
My **toys** are the best presents I ever got.
My favourite person is **Mahi**, who is a gem,
So this, my first poem, is just for them!

Lara Gagneja (4)
Fountain Montessori Preschool, Edgware

Darah's First Poem

My name is Darah and I go to preschool,
My best friend is Lara, who is really cool.
I watch Peppa Pig on TV,
Playing PAW Patrol is lots of fun for me.
I just love chicken to eat,
And sometimes chocolate for a treat.
Pink is a colour I like a lot,
My teddy bear is the best present I ever got.
My favourite person is Mummy, who is a gem,
So this, my first poem, is just for them!

Darah Uloroh (4)
Fountain Montessori Preschool, Edgware

Daniel's First Poem

My name is Daniel and I go to preschool,
My best friend is Vedant, who is really cool.
I watch PAW Patrol on TV,
Playing with toys is lots of fun for me.
I just love food to eat,
And sometimes chocolate for a treat.
Red is a colour I like a lot,
My racing car is the best present I ever got.
My favourite person is Daddy, who is a gem,
So this, my first poem, is just for them!

Daniel Rafael Lavric (3)
Fountain Montessori Preschool, Edgware

Sarah's First Poem

My name is Sarah and I go to preschool,
My best friend is Krish, who is really cool.
I watch Peppa Pig on TV,
Playing football is lots of fun for me.
I just love orange to eat,
And sometimes pink crisps for a treat.
Pink is a colour I like a lot,
My Elsa is the best present I ever got.
My favourite person is Mummy, who is a gem,
So this, my first poem, is just for them!

Sarah Cherifi (4)
Fountain Montessori Preschool, Edgware

Ria's First Poem

My name is **Ria** and I go to preschool,
My best friend is **Mia**, who is really cool.
I watch **Peppa Pig** on TV,
Playing **puzzles** is lots of fun for me.
I just love **chocolate** to eat,
And sometimes **lollipops** for a treat.
Pink is a colour I like a lot,
My **teddy** is the best present I ever got.
My favourite person is **Reya**, who is a gem,
So this, my first poem, is just for them!

Ria Vaghjiani (4)
Fountain Montessori Preschool, Edgware

Shakiel's First Poem

My name is Shakiel and I go to preschool,
My best friend is Ryan, who is really cool.
I watch Andy's Dinosaur Adventures on TV,
Playing trains, cars and dinosaurs is lots of fun for me.
I just love salmon to eat,
And sometimes chocolate ice cream for a treat.
Yellow is a colour I like a lot,
My box of dinosaurs is the best present I ever got.
My favourite person is Daddy, who is a gem,
So this, my first poem, is just for them!

Shakiel Qayyum (3)
Kidz Kabin @ Fortismere, London

Alexandros' First Poem

My name is **Alexandros** and I go to preschool,
My best friend is **Shakiel**, who is really cool.
I watch **PAW Patrol** on TV,
Playing **with balls** is lots of fun for me.
I just love **sausages and toast** to eat,
And sometimes **chocolate ice cream** for a treat.
Blue is a colour I like a lot,
My **big world puzzle** is the best present I ever got.
My favourite person is **Daddy**, who is a gem,
So this, my first poem, is just for them!

Alexandros McDermott (4)
Kidz Kabin @ Fortismere, London

Peggy's First Poem

My name is **Peggy** and I go to preschool,
My best friend is **Maya S**, who is really cool.
I watch **Mister Maker** on TV,
Playing **with Aquabeads** is lots of fun for me.
I just love **banana cake** to eat,
And sometimes **presents** for a treat.
Gold is a colour I like a lot,
My **fairy picture** is the best present I ever got.
My favourite person is **Isabel**, who is a gem,
So this, my first poem, is just for them!

Peggy Kaye (4)
Kidz Kabin @ Fortismere, London

Mazzie's First Poem

My name is **Mazzie** and I go to preschool,
My best friend is **Tatiana**, who is really cool.
I watch **Ben & Holly** on TV,
Playing **in my car** is lots of fun for me.
I just love **mash** to eat,
And sometimes **animal biscuits** for a treat.
Yellow is a colour I like a lot,
My **teddy** is the best present I ever got.
My favourite person is **Mummy**, who is a gem,
So this, my first poem, is just for them!

Mazzie Chambers (4)
Kidz Kabin @ Fortismere, London

Jaia's First Poem

My name is **Jaia** and I go to preschool,
My best friend is **Maisy**, who is really cool.
I watch **Octonauts** on TV,
Playing **princesses** is lots of fun for me.
I just love **broccoli** to eat,
And sometimes **ice cream** for a treat.
Orange is a colour I like a lot,
My **ponies** are the best present I ever got.
My favourite person is **Mummy**, who is a gem,
So this, my first poem, is just for them!

Jaia Slade (4)
Kidz Kabin @ Fortismere, London

Tatiana's First Poem

My name is **Tatiana** and I go to preschool,
My best friend is **Taia**, who is really cool.
I watch **Peppa** on TV,
Playing **with Bob the cat** is lots of fun for me.
I just love **cucumber** to eat,
And sometimes **ice cream** for a treat.
Red is a colour I like a lot,
My **dinosaur** is the best present I ever got.
My favourite person is **Sasha**, who is a gem,
So this, my first poem, is just for them!

Tatiana Gurevich (4)
Kidz Kabin @ Fortismere, London

Hin's First Poem

My name is **Hin** and I go to preschool,
My best friend is **Daddy**, who is really cool.
I watch **Marble Mazes** on TV,
Playing **cars** is lots of fun for me.
I just love **sweetcorn** to eat,
And sometimes **orange** for a treat.
Yellow is a colour I like a lot,
My **car** is the best present I ever got.
My favourite person is **Kurtis**, who is a gem,
So this, my first poem, is just for them!

Hin Van Der Linden (3)
Kidz Kabin @ Fortismere, London

Oliver's First Poem

My name is Oliver and I go to preschool,
My best friend is Huey, who is really cool.
I watch The Numtums on TV,
Playing basketball is lots of fun for me.
I just love potatoes and carrots to eat,
And sometimes a chocolate bar for a treat.
Pink is a colour I like a lot,
My train truck is the best present I ever got.
My favourite person is Grandma, who is a gem,
So this, my first poem, is just for them!

Oliver Balsiger (4)
Kidz Kabin @ Pembroke Studios, London

My First Poem 2017 - North London

Wojciech's First Poem

My name is Wojciech and I go to preschool,
My best friend is Noah, who is really cool.
I watch Curious George on TV,
Playing with Lego is lots of fun for me.
I just love nuggets to eat,
And sometimes ice cream for a treat.
Blue is a colour I like a lot,
My astronaut costume is the best present
I ever got.
My favourite person is Mummy, who is a gem,
So this, my first poem, is just for them!

Wojciech Karwecki (4)
Kidz Kabin @ Pembroke Studios, London

Noah's First Poem

My name is Noah and I go to preschool,
My best friend is Darshan, who is really cool.
I watch Power Rangers on TV,
Playing aeroplanes is lots of fun for me.
I just love pizza to eat,
And sometimes chocolate for a treat.
Blue is a colour I like a lot,
My Spider-Man is the best present I ever got.
My favourite person is Mummy, who is a gem,
So this, my first poem, is just for them!

Noah Bardsley (4)
Kidz Kabin @ Pembroke Studios, London

George's First Poem

My name is **George** and I go to preschool,
My best friend is **Mia K**, who is really cool.
I watch **Thomas the Tank Engine** on TV,
Playing **with Lego** is lots of fun for me.
I just love **toast** to eat,
And sometimes **sweets** for a treat.
Blue is a colour I like a lot,
My **flying car** is the best present I ever got.
My favourite person is **Mummy**, who is a gem,
So this, my first poem, is just for them!

George Coulson (4)
Kidz Kabin @ Pembroke Studios, London

Niamh's First Poem

My name is Niamh and I go to preschool,
My best friend is Hannah, who is really cool.
I watch Frozen on TV,
Playing Barbie is lots of fun for me.
I just love pasta to eat,
And sometimes sweeties for a treat.
Pink is a colour I like a lot,
My hairdresser set is the best present I ever got.
My favourite person is Keir, my brother, who is a gem,
So this, my first poem, is just for them!

Niamh Bird (4)
Kidz Kabin @ Pembroke Studios, London

Huey's First Poem

My name is **Huey** and I go to preschool,
My best friend is **Hugo**, who is really cool.
I watch **Transformers** on TV,
Playing **cars** is lots of fun for me.
I just love **chicken and potatoes** to eat,
And sometimes **chocolate** for a treat.
Brown is a colour I like a lot,
My **scooter** is the best present I ever got.
My favourite person is **Daddy**, who is a gem,
So this, my first poem, is just for them!

Huey Beck (4)
Kidz Kabin @ Pembroke Studios, London

Oliver's First Poem

My name is Oliver and I go to preschool,
My best friend is Abigail, who is really cool.
I watch The Big Bad Wolf on TV,
Playing animals is lots of fun for me.
I just love sausages to eat,
And sometimes ice cream for a treat.
Pink is a colour I like a lot,
My toy car is the best present I ever got.
My favourite person is Daddy, who is a gem,
So this, my first poem, is just for them!

Oliver Birdsey (3)
Kidz Kabin @ Pembroke Studios, London

Ioav's First Poem

My name is **Ioav** and I go to preschool,
My best friend is **Daria**, who is really cool.
I watch **The Numtums** on TV,
Playing **dinosaurs** is lots of fun for me.
I just love **spaghetti** to eat,
And sometimes **a lollipop** for a treat.
Orange is a colour I like a lot,
My **big tractor** is the best present I ever got.
My favourite person is **Nava**, who is a gem,
So this, my first poem, is just for them!

Ioav Baldwin (4)
Kidz Kabin @ Pembroke Studios, London

Darshan's First Poem

My name is **Darshan** and I go to preschool,
My best friend is **Wojciech**, who is really cool.
I watch **Fireman Sam** on TV,
Playing **cars** is lots of fun for me.
I just love **chicken** to eat,
And sometimes **chocolate** for a treat.
Red is a colour I like a lot,
My **blue Spider-Man** is the best present I ever got.
My favourite person is **Noah**, who is a gem,
So this, my first poem, is just for them!

Darshan Iyngkaran (4)
Kidz Kabin @ Pembroke Studios, London

Vian's First Poem

My name is Vian and I go to preschool,
My best friend is Vernel, who is really cool.
I watch Peppa Pig on TV,
Playing with Play-Doh is lots of fun for me.
I just love rice and chicken to eat,
And sometimes sweets for a treat.
Brown is a colour I like a lot,
My toy is the best present I ever got.
My favourite person is Mummy, who is a gem,
So this, my first poem, is just for them!

Vian Matovu (3)
Kidz Kabin @ Pembroke Studios, London

Liam's First Poem

My name is Liam and I go to preschool,
My best friend is Darshan, who is really cool.
I watch movies on TV,
Playing football is lots of fun for me.
I just love sausages to eat,
And sometimes chocolate for a treat.
Green is a colour I like a lot,
My BB-8 is the best present I ever got.
My favourite people are my family, who are gems,
So this, my first poem, is just for them!

Liam Edwards (3)
Kidz Kabin @ Pembroke Studios, London

Vernel's First Poem

My name is **Vernel** and I go to preschool,
My best friend is **Vian**, who is really cool.
I watch **Peppa Pig** on TV,
Playing **dressing up** is lots of fun for me.
I just love **chicken and rice** to eat,
And sometimes **chocolate** for a treat.
Red is a colour I like a lot,
My **toy** is the best present I ever got.
My favourite person is **Mummy**, who is a gem,
So this, my first poem, is just for them!

Vernel Matovu (3)
Kidz Kabin @ Pembroke Studios, London

Kaan's First Poem

My name is **Kaan** and I go to preschool,
My best friend is **Freya**, who is really cool.
I watch **Peppa Pig** on TV,
Playing **cutting and building** is lots of fun for me.
I just love **pasta** to eat,
And sometimes **chocolate** for a treat.
Green is a colour I like a lot,
My **toy** is the best present I ever got.
My favourite person is **Mummy**, who is a gem,
So this, my first poem, is just for them!

Kaan Erdem (4)
Kidz Kabin @ Pembroke Studios, London

Ruby's First Poem

My name is Ruby and I go to preschool,
My best friend is Abigail, who is really cool.
I watch Peppa Pig on TV,
Playing doctors is lots of fun for me.
I just love everything to eat,
And sometimes chocolate cake for a treat.
Green is a colour I like a lot,
My doll is the best present I ever got.
My favourite person is Mummy, who is a gem,
So this, my first poem, is just for them!

Ruby Ayetigbo-Bamgbose (4)
Kidz Kabin @ Pembroke Studios, London

Elai's First Poem

My name is Elai and I go to preschool,
My best friend is Darshan, who is really cool.
I watch Star Wars on TV,
Playing with Lego is lots of fun for me.
I just love pizza to eat,
And sometimes chocolate for a treat.
Blue is a colour I like a lot,
My Stormtooper is the best present I ever got.
My favourite person is Gideon, who is a gem,
So this, my first poem, is just for them!

Elai Ben Ari (4)
Kidz Kabin @ Pembroke Studios, London

Amiya's First Poem

My name is **Amiya** and I go to preschool,
My best friend is **Hannah**, who is really cool.
I watch **Peppa Pig** on TV,
Playing **Happy Families** is lots of fun for me.
I just love **olives** to eat,
And sometimes **sweets** for a treat.
Pink is a colour I like a lot,
My **flap book** is the best present I ever got.
My favourite person is **Shrey**, who is a gem,
So this, my first poem, is just for them!

Amiya Fakey (3)
Kidz Kabin @ Pembroke Studios, London

Violet's First Poem

My name is **Violet** and I go to preschool,
My best friend is **Mia K**, who is really cool.
I watch **The Numtums** on TV,
Playing **with Lego** is lots of fun for me.
I just love **pasta** to eat,
And sometimes **sweets** for a treat.
Blue is a colour I like a lot,
My **cash register** is the best present I ever got.
My favourite person is **Mummy**, who is a gem,
So this, my first poem, is just for them!

Violet Foran (3)
Kidz Kabin @ Pembroke Studios, London

Daria's First Poem

My name is Daria and I go to preschool,
My best friend is Ioav, who is really cool.
I watch PAW Patrol on TV,
Playing dressing up is lots of fun for me.
I just love spaghetti to eat,
And sometimes lollipops for a treat.
Pink is a colour I like a lot,
My Barbie is the best present I ever got.
My favourite person is Mummy, who is a gem,
So this, my first poem, is just for them!

Daria Sgnaolin (4)
Kidz Kabin @ Pembroke Studios, London

Kianna's First Poem

My name is **Kianna** and I go to preschool,
My best friend is **Precious**, who is really cool.
I watch **Peppa Pig** on TV,
Playing **with Play-Doh** is lots of fun for me.
I just love **pasta** to eat,
And sometimes **chocolate** for a treat.
Red is a colour I like a lot,
My **toy** is the best present I ever got.
My favourite person is **Mummy**, who is a gem,
So this, my first poem, is just for them!

Kianna George (4)
Kidz Kabin @ Pembroke Studios, London

Zara's First Poem

My name is Zara and I go to preschool,
My best friend is Daria, who is really cool.
I watch Frozen on TV,
Playing dressing up is lots of fun for me.
I just love pasta to eat,
And sometimes chocolate for a treat.
Pink is a colour I like a lot,
My princess toy is the best present I ever got.
My favourite person is Daddy, who is a gem,
So this, my first poem, is just for them!

Zara Beresford (4)
Kidz Kabin @ Pembroke Studios, London

Maggie's First Poem

My name is **Maggie** and I go to preschool,
My best friend is **Abigail**, who is really cool.
I watch **Peppa Pig** on TV,
Playing **dollies** is lots of fun for me.
I just love **pasta** to eat,
And sometimes **cake** for a treat.
Purple is a colour I like a lot,
My **Elsa dress** is the best present I ever got.
My favourite person is **Mummy**, who is a gem,
So this, my first poem, is just for them!

Maggie McLean (4)
Kidz Kabin @ Pembroke Studios, London

Mia's First Poem

My name is **Mia** and I go to preschool,
My best friend is **Mia K**, who is really cool.
I watch **Peppa Pig** on TV,
Playing **with Duplo** is lots of fun for me.
I just love **egg** to eat,
And sometimes **chocolate** for a treat.
Red is a colour I like a lot,
My **scooter** is the best present I ever got.
My favourite person is **my sister**, who is a gem,
So this, my first poem, is just for them!

Mia Scarso Borioli (3)
Kidz Kabin @ Pembroke Studios, London

Oscar's First Poem

My name is Oscar and I go to preschool,
My best friend is Mia SB, who is really cool.
I watch Peppa Pig on TV,
Playing with sand is lots of fun for me.
I just love pizza to eat,
And sometimes chocolate for a treat.
Green is a colour I like a lot,
My toy is the best present I ever got.
My favourite person is Mummy, who is a gem,
So this, my first poem, is just for them!

Oscar Du Rose (3)
Kidz Kabin @ Pembroke Studios, London

Erin's First Poem

My name is Erin and I go to preschool,
My best friend is Mummy, who is really cool.
I watch Peppa Pig on TV,
Playing Fireman Sam is lots of fun for me.
I just love pasta to eat,
And sometimes cake for a treat.
Green is a colour I like a lot,
My toy cat is the best present I ever got.
My favourite person is Mummy, who is a gem,
So this, my first poem, is just for them!

Erin Henson (3)
Kidz Kabin @ Pembroke Studios, London

George's First Poem

My name is George and I go to preschool,
My best friend is Caroline, who is really cool.
I watch The Numtums on TV,
Playing out is lots of fun for me.
I just love pizza to eat,
And sometimes sweets for a treat.
Blue is a colour I like a lot,
My toy is the best present I ever got.
My favourite person is Mummy, who is a gem,
So this, my first poem, is just for them!

George Love (3)
Kidz Kabin @ Pembroke Studios, London

Freya's First Poem

My name is Freya and I go to preschool,
My best friend is Kaan, who is really cool.
I watch Peppa Pig on TV,
Playing with sand is lots of fun for me.
I just love pizza to eat,
And sometimes cake for a treat.
Pink is a colour I like a lot,
My toy is the best present I ever got.
My favourite person is Mummy, who is a gem,
So this, my first poem, is just for them!

Freya Erdem (4)
Kidz Kabin @ Pembroke Studios, London

Jacob's First Poem

My name is Jacob and I go to preschool,
My best friend is Sianny, who is really cool.
I watch Blaze and the Monster Machines on TV,
Playing cars is lots of fun for me.
I just love salmon and rice to eat,
And sometimes carrot cake for a treat.
Orange is a colour I like a lot,
My scooter is the best present I ever got.
My favourite people are Mummy and Mama, who are gems,
So this, my first poem, is just for them!

Jacob Corrigan (3)
Little Angels Schoolhouse, London

Jahmal's First Poem

My name is Jahmal and I go to preschool,
My best friend is Zakai, who is really cool.
I watch Peppa Pig on TV,
Playing on a Spider-Man motorbike is lots of fun for me.
I just love fruit and grapes to eat,
And sometimes strawberries and cake for a treat.
Purple is a colour I like a lot,
My fire engine is the best present I ever got.
My favourite person is Mummy, who is a gem,
So this, my first poem, is just for them!

Jahmal Aston Walker-Stewart (2)
Little Angels Schoolhouse, London

Hector's First Poem

My name is Hector and I go to preschool,
My best friends are Paul and Marcos, who are really cool.
I watch PAW Patrol on TV,
Playing puzzles and cars is lots of fun for me.
I just love Weetabix to eat,
And sometimes chocolate for a treat.
Blue is a colour I like a lot,
My PAW Patrol puzzle is the best present I ever got.
My favourite person is Rosa, who is a gem,
So this, my first poem, is just for them!

Hector (3)
Little Angels Schoolhouse, London

Olamide's First Poem

My name is **Olamide** and I go to preschool,
My best friend is **Lily-May**, who is really cool.
I watch **Power Rangers** on TV,
Playing **football** is lots of fun for me.
I just love **spaghetti Bolognese** to eat,
And sometimes **chocolate** for a treat.
Red is a colour I like a lot,
My **Power Rangers watch** is the best present I ever got.
My favourite person is **my mummy**, who is a gem,
So this, my first poem, is just for them!

Olamide Bickersteth (4)
Little Angels Schoolhouse, London

Rufus' First Poem

My name is Rufus and I go to preschool,
My best friend is Arnold, who is really cool.
I watch the Cars movie on TV,
Playing cars, cars, cars is lots of fun for me.
I just love lots of things to eat,
And sometimes chocolate for a treat.
Reddy, reddy red is a colour I like a lot,
My Lego is the best present I ever got.
My favourite person is my sister Hilda, who is a gem,
So this, my first poem, is just for them!

Rufus Edwin Finch (3)
Little Angels Schoolhouse, London

Aiden's First Poem

My name is Aiden and I go to preschool,
My best friend is Iris, who is really cool.
I watch PAW Patrol on TV,
Playing cars is lots of fun for me.
I just love ice cream to eat,
And sometimes lollipops for a treat.
Blue is a colour I like a lot,
My trains are the best present I ever got.
My favourite people are my mummy and baby sister Mia, who are gems,
So this, my first poem, is just for them!

Aiden Kyle Samuel-Maraj (4)
Little Angels Schoolhouse, London

Arman's First Poem

My name is **Arman** and I go to preschool,
My best friends are **Asher and Alexander**, who are really cool.
I watch **Peppa Pig** on TV,
Playing **with Lego** is lots of fun for me.
I just love **pasta** to eat,
And sometimes **chocolate** for a treat.
Blue is a colour I like a lot,
My **dinosaur game** is the best present I ever got.
My favourite person is **my dad**, who is a gem,
So this, my first poem, is just for them!

Arman Chajai (3)
Little Angels Schoolhouse, London

My First Poem 2017 - North London

Asher's First Poem

My name is **Asher** and I go to preschool,
My best friend is **Arman**, who is really cool.
I watch **Ninja Turtles** on TV,
Playing **with Ninja Turtle toys** is lots of fun for me.
I just love **spaghetti** to eat,
And sometimes **lollipops** for a treat.
Blue is a colour I like a lot,
My **PAW Patrol toy** is the best present I ever got.
My favourite person is **Grandad**, who is a gem,
So this, my first poem, is just for them!

Asher Brew (3)
Little Angels Schoolhouse, London

Iris' First Poem

My name is **Iris** and I go to preschool,
My best friend is **Arman**, who is really cool.
I watch **Peppa Pig** on TV,
Playing **doctors** is lots of fun for me.
I just love **strawberries** to eat,
And sometimes **sweeties** for a treat.
Pink is a colour I like a lot,
My **'Let It Go' toy** is the best present I ever got.
My favourite person is **my baby**, who is a gem,
So this, my first poem, is just for them!

Iris Zacharladis (3)
Little Angels Schoolhouse, London

Alivia's First Poem

My name is **Alivia** and I go to preschool,
My best friend is **Yaya**, who is really cool.
I watch **PAW Patrol** on TV,
Playing **with Peppa Pig toys** is lots of fun for me.
I just love **chips** to eat,
And sometimes **sweets** for a treat.
Pink is a colour I like a lot,
My **mermaid** is the best present I ever got.
My favourite person is **Mummy**, who is a gem,
So this, my first poem, is just for them!

Alivia Dovies-Mozo (3)
Little Angels Schoolhouse, London

Merryn's First Poem

My name is **Merryn** and I go to preschool,
My best friend is **Rufus**, who is really cool.
I watch **Peter Rabbit** on TV,
Playing **with my teddy** is lots of fun for me.
I just love **pasta** to eat,
And sometimes **sweeties** for a treat.
Yellow is a colour I like a lot,
My **bike** is the best present I ever got.
My favourite person is **Rio**, who is a gem,
So this, my first poem, is just for them!

Merryn Ash (3)
Little Angels Schoolhouse, London

Ishaani's First Poem

My name is Ishaani and I go to preschool,
My best friends are Vihara, Anaya and Isha, who are really cool.
I watch Blaze and the Monster Machines on TV,
Playing with My Little Pony is lots of fun for me.
I just love rice and chicken to eat,
And sometimes chocolate for a treat.
Purple is a colour I like a lot,
My My Little Pony is the best present I ever got.
My favourite people are Mummy and Daddy,
who are gems,
So this, my first poem, is just for them!

Ishaani Mistry (4)
Longfield Primary School, Harrow

Bohanegan's First Poem

My name is **Bohanegan** and I go to preschool,
My best friends are **Lojith and Chenaya**, who are really cool.
I watch **Lego Friends and Big Dora** on TV,
Playing **fire engines and police cars** is lots of fun for me.
I just love **rice and cornflakes** to eat,
And sometimes **chocolate** for a treat.
Red is a colour I like a lot,
My **helicopter with remote** is the best present I ever got.
My favourite people are **my sister and my brother**, who are gems,
So this, my first poem, is just for them!

Bohanegan Senthil (4)
Longfield Primary School, Harrow

Maryam's First Poem

My name is **Maryam** and I go to preschool,
My best friend is **Ziya**, who is really cool.
I watch **Super Wings** on TV,
Playing **with my brother** is lots of fun for me.
I just love **tutti frutti cake** to eat,
And sometimes **grapes** for a treat.
Duck blue is a colour I like a lot,
My **Peppa Pig playset** is the best present I ever got.
My favourite person is **Mohamed Aman**, who is a gem,
So this, my first poem, is just for them!

Maryam Mafaz (4)
Longfield Primary School, Harrow

Khushi's First Poem

My name is **Khushi** and I go to preschool,
My best friend is **Shanaya**, who is really cool.
I watch **Peppa Pig** on TV,
Playing **with my teddy bear** is lots of fun for me.
I just love **noodles** to eat,
And sometimes **chocolate** for a treat.
Pink is a colour I like a lot,
My **doll's house** is the best present I ever got.
My favourite person is **my sister Khushboo**,
who is a gem,
So this, my first poem, is just for them!

Khushi Rashmi Darbar (4)
Longfield Primary School, Harrow

Alisha's First Poem

My name is Alisha and I go to preschool,
My best friend is Mummy, who is really cool.
I watch My Little Pony on TV,
Playing with my toys is lots of fun for me.
I just love pizza to eat,
And sometimes cookies for a treat.
Pink is a colour I like a lot,
My Peppa Pig scooter is the best present I ever got.
My favourite people are Mummy and Daddy,
who are gems,
So this, my first poem, is just for them!

Alisha Mehta (4)
Longfield Primary School, Harrow

Maria's First Poem

My name is Maria and I go to preschool,
My best friend is Sundus, who is really cool.
I watch Shimmer and Shine on TV,
Playing Shimmer and Shine games is lots of fun for me.
I just love noodles to eat,
And sometimes apples and bananas for a treat.
Pink is a colour I like a lot,
My pink iPad is the best present I ever got.
My favourite person is Maryam, who is a gem,
So this, my first poem, is just for them!

Maria Saya (3)
Longfield Primary School, Harrow

Haviya's First Poem

My name is Haviya and I go to preschool,
My best friend is Saara, who is really cool.
I watch Tots TV on TV,
Playing on the swings is lots of fun for me.
I just love chicken to eat,
And sometimes chocolate for a treat.
Pink is a colour I like a lot,
My dog is the best present I ever got.
My favourite person is my cousin 'Chippy',
who is a gem,
So this, my first poem, is just for them!

Haviya Arasenthan (4)
Longfield Primary School, Harrow

Krishan's First Poem

My name is Krishan and I go to preschool,
My best friend is my dad, who is really cool.
I watch Ben & Holly on TV,
Playing cars is lots of fun for me.
I just love broccoli to eat,
And sometimes wheat-free pizza for a treat.
Blue is a colour I like a lot,
My PAW Patrol hat is the best present I ever got.
My favourite person is my mum, who is a gem,
So this, my first poem, is just for them!

Krishan Prem Badhwar (4)

Longfield Primary School, Harrow

Ziya's First Poem

My name is **Ziya** and I go to preschool,
My best friend is **Omie**, who is really cool.
I watch **Peppa Pig** on TV,
Playing **dollies** is lots of fun for me.
I just love **cucumber sandwiches** to eat,
And sometimes **sweets** for a treat.
Purple is a colour I like a lot,
My **brother** is the best present I ever got.
My favourite person is **Krish, my brother**,
who is a gem,
So this, my first poem, is just for them!

Ziya J Patel (4)
Longfield Primary School, Harrow

Ram's First Poem

My name is **Ram** and I go to preschool,
My best friend is **Adam**, who is really cool.
I watch **Peppa Pig** on TV,
Playing **trains** is lots of fun for me.
I just love **spinach** to eat,
And sometimes **chocolate** for a treat.
Purple is a colour I like a lot,
My **aeroplanes** are the best present I ever got.
My favourite person is **my baby, he can walk now**,
who is a gem,
So this, my first poem, is just for them!

Ram Anand Kesar (3)
Longfield Primary School, Harrow

Aarusan's First Poem

My name is **Aarusan** and I go to preschool,
My best friend is **Sibi**, who is really cool.
I watch **Octonauts** on TV,
Playing **PAW Patrol** is lots of fun for me.
I just love **pancakes** to eat,
And sometimes **papaya** for a treat.
Blue is a colour I like a lot,
My **builder, Rubble** is the best present I ever got.
My favourite person is **my Appa**, who is very sweet,
So this, my first poem, is just for them!

Aarusan Mathiyalagkan (4)
Longfield Primary School, Harrow

Vihara's First Poem

My name is Vihara and I go to preschool,
My best friend is Isha, who is really cool.
I watch Peppa Pig on TV,
Playing with Barbie sets is lots of fun for me.
I just love cornflakes to eat,
And sometimes chocolate for a treat.
Pink is a colour I like a lot,
My Barbie is the best present I ever got.
My favourite person is my mummy, who is a gem,
So this, my first poem, is just for them!

Vihara Pakalapati (4)
Longfield Primary School, Harrow

Maizie's First Poem

My name is **Maizie** and I go to preschool,
My best friend is **Lala**, who is really cool.
I watch **Numberblocks** on TV,
Playing **the hippo game** is lots of fun for me.
I just love **Rice Krispies** to eat,
And sometimes **biscuits** for a treat.
Red is a colour I like a lot,
My **pram** is the best present I ever got.
My favourite person is **Mummy**, who is a gem,
So this, my first poem, is just for them!

Maizie Grundy (4)
Longfield Primary School, Harrow

Lily's First Poem

My name is **Lily** and I go to preschool,
My best friend is **Grandad**, who is really cool.
I watch **In the Night Garden** on TV,
Playing **with toys** is lots of fun for me.
I just love **toast** to eat,
And sometimes **yoghurt** for a treat.
Green is a colour I like a lot,
My **scooter** is the best present I ever got.
My favourite person is **Nana**, who is a gem,
So this, my first poem, is just for them!

Lily Gutteridge (4)
Longfield Primary School, Harrow

Lojith's First Poem

My name is Lojith and I go to preschool,
My best friend is Bohan, who is really cool.
I watch PAW Patrol on TV,
Playing cars is lots of fun for me.
I just love chocolate balls to eat,
And sometimes bread for a treat.
Blue is a colour I like a lot,
My telescope is the best present I ever got.
My favourite person is my sister, who is a gem,
So this, my first poem, is just for them!

Lojith Kirishanth (4)
Longfield Primary School, Harrow

Kannisha's First Poem

My name is **Kannisha** and I go to preschool,
My best friend is **my brother**, who is really cool.
I watch **Peppa Pig** on TV,
Playing **car games** is lots of fun for me.
I just love **tomatoes** to eat,
And sometimes **biscuits** for a treat.
Red is a colour I like a lot,
My **doll** is the best present I ever got.
My favourite person is **Grandad**, who is a gem,
So this, my first poem, is just for them!

Kannisha Sobinarth (4)
Longfield Primary School, Harrow

Chenaya's First Poem

My name is Chenaya and I go to preschool,
My best friend is Isha, who is really cool.
I watch Peppa Pig on TV,
Playing dolls is lots of fun for me.
I just love macaroni to eat,
And sometimes chocolate for a treat.
Pink is a colour I like a lot,
My dolls are the best present I ever got.
My favourite person is my sister, who is a gem,
So this, my first poem, is just for them!

Chenaya Rajapaksha (4)
Longfield Primary School, Harrow

Anaya's First Poem

My name is **Anaya** and I go to preschool,
My best friend is **Isha**, who is really cool.
I watch **Peppa Pig** on TV,
Playing **on my scooter** is lots of fun for me.
I just love **carrots** to eat,
And sometimes **chocolate** for a treat.
Pink is a colour I like a lot,
My **Barbie** is the best present I ever got.
My favourite person is **Mummy**, who is a gem,
So this, my first poem, is just for them!

Anaya Bela Patel (3)
Longfield Primary School, Harrow

Jasmin's First Poem

My name is Jasmin and I go to preschool,
My best friend is Kian, who is really cool.
I watch Power Rangers on TV,
Playing dinosaurs is lots of fun for me.
I just love hot dogs to eat,
And sometimes lollies for a treat.
Blue is a colour I like a lot,
My Aria is the best present I ever got.
My favourite person is Mummy, who is a gem,
So this, my first poem, is just for them!

Jasmin Sehdev (4)
Longfield Primary School, Harrow

Thasvin's First Poem

My name is Thasvin and I go to preschool,
My best friend is Lojith, who is really cool.
I watch superheroes on TV,
Playing cars is lots of fun for me.
I just love pasta to eat,
And sometimes fruit for a treat.
Blue is a colour I like a lot,
My toy train is the best present I ever got.
My favourite person is my dad, who is a gem,
So this, my first poem, is just for them!

Thasvin Vijayatharan (4)
Longfield Primary School, Harrow

Kian's First Poem

My name is Kian and I go to preschool,
My best friend is Izaan, who is really cool.
I watch The Numtums on TV,
Playing cars is lots of fun for me.
I just love chicken to eat,
And sometimes lemon cake for a treat.
Red is a colour I like a lot,
My car is the best present I ever got.
My favourite person is my mum, who is a gem,
So this, my first poem, is just for them!

Kian Borkhataria (4)
Longfield Primary School, Harrow

Kian's First Poem

My name is **Kian** and I go to preschool,
My best friend is **Abeer**, who is really cool.
I watch **ponies** on TV,
Playing **trains** is lots of fun for me.
I just love **cake** to eat,
And sometimes **chocolate** for a treat.
Red is a colour I like a lot,
My **scooter** is the best present I ever got.
My favourite person is **Daddy**, who is a gem,
So this, my first poem, is just for them!

Kian Wong (3)
Longfield Primary School, Harrow

Adam's First Poem

My name is Adam and I go to preschool,
My best friends are Jake and Mila, who are really cool.
I watch Batman on TV,
Playing with little Lego is lots of fun for me.
I just love meatballs to eat,
And sometimes chocolate buttons for a treat.
Blue is a colour I like a lot,
My Batman is the best present I ever got.
My favourite person is Katie, who is a gem,
So this, my first poem, is just for them!

Adam David Humphreys (4)
Platform One Nursery, London

Eliz's First Poem

My name is Eliz and I go to preschool,
My best friend is Sophie, who is really cool.
I watch PAW Patrol on TV,
Playing role play babies is lots of fun for me.
I just love vegetables to eat,
And sometimes chocolate for a treat.
Blue is a colour I like a lot,
My pink dress is the best present I ever got.
My favourite person is Mummy, who is a gem,
So this, my first poem, is just for them!

Eliz Sevin Sarak (3)
Platform One Nursery, London

Lara's First Poem

My name is **Lara** and I go to preschool,
My best friend is **Mila**, who is really cool.
I watch **PAW Patrol** on TV,
Playing **farm animals** is lots of fun for me.
I just love **roast dinners** to eat,
And sometimes **sweeties** for a treat.
Yellow is a colour I like a lot,
My **unicorn** is the best present I ever got.
My favourite person is **Mummy**, who is a gem,
So this, my first poem, is just for them!

Lara Cristina Coles (3)
Platform One Nursery, London

Sam's First Poem

My name is Sam and I go to preschool,
My best friend is Jake, who is really cool.
I watch Batman on TV,
Playing dinosaurs is lots of fun for me.
I just love bread to eat,
And sometimes cake for a treat.
Red is a colour I like a lot,
My ice cave is the best present I ever got.
My favourite person is Batman, who is a gem,
So this, my first poem, is just for them!

Sam Bedworth (3)
Platform One Nursery, London

Eva's First Poem

My name is Eva and I go to preschool,
My best friend is Isabella, who is really cool.
I watch Peppa Pig on TV,
Playing with my mummy and daddy is lots of fun for me.
I just love my mummy's spaghetti to eat,
And sometimes an Elsa chocolate for a treat.
Blue is a colour I like a lot,
My Barbie doll is the best present I ever got.
My favourite people are Daddy Isabella and Mummy, who are gems,
So this, my first poem, is just for them!

Eva Bauzaite (4)
Puddleducks Nursery, London

Benicio's First Poem

My name is Benicio and I go to preschool,
My best friend is David, who is really cool.
I watch Ben & Holly on TV,
Playing with Play-Doh is lots of fun for me.
I just love fish and chips to eat,
And sometimes chocolate for a treat.
Purple is a colour I like a lot,
My bike is the best present I ever got.
My favourite person is Alicia, who is a gem,
So this, my first poem, is just for them!

Benicio Laurnagaray (3)
Puddleducks Nursery, London

Abiyah's First Poem

My name is **Abiyah** and I go to preschool,
My best friends are **Darius and Ojoma**, who are really cool.
I watch **Sofia the First** on TV,
Playing **hide-and-seek** is lots of fun for me.
I just love **noodles** to eat,
And sometimes **strawberry ice cream** for a treat.
Pink is a colour I like a lot,
My **Frozen plate and Frozen cup** are the best presents I ever got.
My favourite people are **my family**, who are gems,
So this, my first poem, is just for them!

Abiyah Adebayo (4)
Raynham Primary School - Edmonton Nursery, London

Angelica's First Poem

My name is **Angelica** and I go to preschool,
My best friends are **Raisa and Maya**, who are really cool.
I watch **Peppa Pig** on TV,
Playing **with my spinner toy** is lots of fun for me.
I just love **bread and chocolate spread** to eat,
And sometimes **chocolate ice cream** for a treat.
Brown is a colour I like a lot,
My **butterfly dolly** is the best present I ever got.
My favourite person is **Mumma**, who is a gem,
So this, my first poem, is just for them!

Angelica Nyang (4)
Raynham Primary School - Edmonton Nursery, London

Janelle's First Poem

My name is **Janelle** and I go to preschool,
My best friend is **Mari**, who is really cool.
I watch **Elsa** on TV,
Playing **with my toys with my sister** is lots of fun for me.
I just love **sausage with pasta** to eat,
And sometimes **marshmallows** for a treat.
Pink is a colour I like a lot,
My **Elsa toy from the beach** is the best present I ever got.
My favourite people are **Mummy, Daddy and Mikah**, who are gems,
So this, my first poem, is just for them!

Janelle Ajayi-Gabriel (4)
Raynham Primary School - Edmonton Nursery, London

Zander's First Poem

My name is Zander and I go to preschool,
My best friend is Mahdi, who is really cool.
I watch lots of things on TV,
Playing in the park is lots of fun for me.
I just love meatballs with chips to eat,
And sometimes vanilla ice cream for a treat.
Orange is a colour I like a lot,
My Minions skateboard is the best present
I ever got.
My favourite people are my mummy and daddy,
who are gems,
So this, my first poem, is just for them!

Zander Basson (4)
Raynham Primary School - Edmonton Nursery, London

Prince's First Poem

My name is Prince and I go to preschool,
My best friend is Tomide, who is really cool.
I watch Peppa Pig on TV,
Playing football is lots of fun for me.
I just love chicken and chips to eat,
And sometimes strawberry ice cream for a treat.
Red is a colour I like a lot,
My teddy bear is the best present I ever got.
My favourite people are Daddy and Phillip,
who are gems,
So this, my first poem, is just for them!

Prince Owusu Appiah Opokuware (3)
Raynham Primary School - Edmonton Nursery, London

Eyasu's First Poem

My name is **Eyasu** and I go to preschool,
My best friend is **Berat**, who is really cool.
I watch **Power Rangers** on TV,
Playing **football** is lots of fun for me.
I just love **cheese sandwiches** to eat,
And sometimes **strawberry ice cream** for a treat.
Blue is a colour I like a lot,
My **PAW Patrol** is the best present I ever got.
My favourite person is **Fortuna, my sister**,
who is a gem,
So this, my first poem, is just for them!

Eyasu Tesfaldet (4)
Raynham Primary School - Edmonton Nursery, London

Dion's First Poem

My name is Dion and I go to preschool,
My best friend is Matilda, who is really cool.
I watch Peppa Pig on TV,
Playing in the fun house is lots of fun for me.
I just love pizza to eat,
And sometimes yoghurt, banana flavour
for a treat.
Blue is a colour I like a lot,
My Christmas toys are the best presents I ever got.
My favourite person is Daddy, who is a gem,
So this, my first poem, is just for them!

Dion Restelica (3)
Raynham Primary School - Edmonton Nursery, London

Bonnie's First Poem

My name is Bonnie and I go to preschool,
My best friend is Ahmed, who is really cool.
I watch CBeebies on TV,
Playing with my brother and sister is lots of fun for me.
I just love pasta to eat,
And sometimes yoghurt, my favourite, strawberry for a treat.
Pink is a colour I like a lot,
My buggy is the best present I ever got.
My favourite person is Mummy, who is a gem,
So this, my first poem, is just for them!

Bonnie Edwards (3)

Raynham Primary School – Edmonton Nursery, London

Khalia's First Poem

My name is Khalia and I go to preschool,
My best friend is Elnaz, who is really cool.
I watch Peppa Pig on TV,
Playing games with my little brother is lots of fun for me.
I just love cereal, Cornflakes to eat,
And sometimes chocolate for a treat.
Pink is a colour I like a lot,
My buggy is the best present I ever got.
My favourite person is Grandma, who is a gem,
So this, my first poem, is just for them!

Khalia Archer (3)
Raynham Primary School - Edmonton Nursery, London

Charlie's First Poem

My name is Charlie and I go to preschool,
My best friend is Omar, who is really cool.
I watch football on TV,
Playing on the climbing frame is lots of fun for me.
I just love breakfast, Weetabix, to eat,
And sometimes chocolate for a treat.
Yellow is a colour I like a lot,
My red car is the best present I ever got.
My favourite person is Daddy, who is a gem,
So this, my first poem, is just for them!

Charlie Savva (4)
Raynham Primary School - Edmonton Nursery, London

Mahdi's First Poem

My name is Mahdi and I go to preschool,
My best friend is Zander, who is really cool.
I watch Spider-Man on TV,
Playing bicycle is lots of fun for me.
I just love spaghetti to eat,
And sometimes strawberry ice cream for a treat.
Green is a colour I like a lot,
My Spider-Man suit is the best present I ever got.
My favourite person is Mummy, who is a gem,
So this, my first poem, is just for them!

Mahdi Muhamed (4)
Raynham Primary School - Edmonton Nursery, London

Stefania's First Poem

My name is **Stefania** and I go to preschool,
My best friend is **Aylin**, who is really cool.
I watch **Barbie** on TV,
Playing **in a car** is lots of fun for me.
I just love **soup** to eat,
And sometimes **ice cream** for a treat.
Purple is a colour I like a lot,
My **dolly sleeping baby** is the best present
I ever got.
My favourite person is **Daddy**, who is a gem,
So this, my first poem, is just for them!

Stefania Elisa Craciun (4)
Raynham Primary School - Edmonton Nursery, London

Cianna's First Poem

My name is Cianna and I go to preschool,
My best friend is Mari, who is really cool.
I watch Peppa Pig on TV,
Playing with my toys, my baby is lots of fun for me.
I just love pizza to eat,
And sometimes jelly for a treat.
Green is a colour I like a lot,
My buggy is the best present I ever got.
My favourite person is my sister Renika, who is a gem,
So this, my first poem, is just for them!

Cianna Pearce (4)
Raynham Primary School – Edmonton Nursery, London

Lucca's First Poem

My name is **Lucca** and I go to preschool,
My best friend is **Aylin**, who is really cool.
I watch **Mickey Mouse** on TV,
Playing **Marble Run** is lots of fun for me.
I just love **a sausage roll** to eat,
And sometimes **a cupcake** for a treat.
Pink is a colour I like a lot,
My **laptop** is the best present I ever got.
My favourite person is **Grandad**, who is a gem,
So this, my first poem, is just for them!

Lucca Christos Asaad-Morcos (3)
Raynham Primary School – Edmonton Nursery, London

Berat's First Poem

My name is **Berat** and I go to preschool,
My best friend is **Eyasu**, who is really cool.
I watch **Tweenies** on TV,
Playing **football** is lots of fun for me.
I just love **pasta** to eat,
And sometimes **chocolate** for a treat.
Red is a colour I like a lot,
My **big, blue car** is the best present I ever got.
My favourite person is **my brother Yigit**, who is a gem,
So this, my first poem, is just for them!

Berat Ergun (4)
Raynham Primary School – Edmonton Nursery, London

Mari's First Poem

My name is Mari and I go to preschool,
My best friend is Janelle, who is really cool.
I watch Peppa Pig on TV,
Playing on my bike is lots of fun for me.
I just love pizza to eat,
And sometimes ice cream for a treat.
Red is a colour I like a lot,
My Sofia the First is the best present I ever got.
My favourite person is Grandad, who is a gem,
So this, my first poem, is just for them!

Mari Smith-Addis (4)
Raynham Primary School - Edmonton Nursery, London

Ojoma's First Poem

My name is Ojoma and I go to preschool,
My best friend is Darius, who is really cool.
I watch CBeebies on TV,
Playing hide-and-seek is lots of fun for me.
I just love spaghetti to eat,
And sometimes ice cream for a treat.
Pink is a colour I like a lot,
My teddy bear is the best present I ever got.
My favourite person is Daddy, who is a gem,
So this, my first poem, is just for them!

Ojoma Onoji (3)
Raynham Primary School - Edmonton Nursery, London

George's First Poem

My name is George and I go to preschool,
My best friends are Josephine, Vivienne and Ariya, who are really cool.
I watch PAW Patrol on TV,
Playing cars is lots of fun for me.
I just love Weetabix and toast to eat,
And sometimes Haribos for a treat.
Yellow is a colour I like a lot,
My robot is the best present I ever got.
My favourite people are my nanny and grandpa, who are gems,
So this, my first poem, is just for them!

George Simpson (4)
Scribbles Nursery, London

Jennifer's First Poem

My name is Jennifer and I go to preschool,
My best friend is Silver, who is really cool.
I watch PAW Patrol on TV,
Playing with my doll's house is lots of fun for me.
I just love pasta pesto to eat,
And sometimes chocolate for a treat.
Pink is a colour I like a lot,
My Peppa Pig is the best present I ever got.
My favourite people are family, who are gems,
So this, my first poem, is just for them!

Jennifer Kane (3)
Scribbles Nursery, London

Alexander's First Poem

My name is **Alexander** and I go to preschool,
My best friends are **Jack and Christian**, who are really cool.
I watch **Peter Rabbit** on TV,
Playing **cars** is lots of fun for me.
I just love **pizza** to eat,
And sometimes **chocolate** for a treat.
Orange is a colour I like a lot,
My **T-rex** is the best present I ever got.
My favourite person is **Daddy**, who is a gem,
So this, my first poem, is just for them!

Alexander Quinto (4)
Scribbles Nursery, London

Josephine's First Poem

My name is Josephine and I go to preschool,
My best friend is Victor, who is really cool.
I watch PAW Patrol on TV,
Playing Barbies is lots of fun for me.
I just love cheesy pasta to eat,
And sometimes sweeties for a treat.
Pink is a colour I like a lot,
My big Barbies are the best present I ever got.
My favourite person is Mummy, who is a gem,
So this, my first poem, is just for them!

Josephine Orczyk (4)
Scribbles Nursery, London

Vivienne's First Poem

My name is **Vivienne** and I go to preschool,
My best friend is **George**, who is really cool.
I watch **PJ Masks** on TV,
Playing **Barbies** is lots of fun for me.
I just love **spaghetti meatballs** to eat,
And sometimes **sweets** for a treat.
Red is a colour I like a lot,
My **buzzy bee** is the best present I ever got.
My favourite person is **George**, who is a gem,
So this, my first poem, is just for them!

Vivienne O'Shea (3)
Scribbles Nursery, London

Sebastian's First Poem

My name is Sebastian and I go to preschool,
My best friend is Mummy, who is really cool.
I watch Go Jetters on TV,
Playing PAW Patrol is lots of fun for me.
I just love mashed potato to eat,
And sometimes smoothies for a treat.
Rainbow is a colour I like a lot,
My fire engine is the best present I ever got.
My favourite person is Joshua, who is a gem,
So this, my first poem, is just for them!

Sebastian Haward (3)
Scribbles Nursery, London

Damon's First Poem

My name is Damon and I go to preschool,
My best friend is Henry, who is really cool.
I watch dinosaurs on TV,
Playing dinosaurs is lots of fun for me.
I just love sausages to eat,
And sometimes chocolate for a treat.
Orange is a colour I like a lot,
My dinosaurs are the best present I ever got.
My favourite person is Daddy, who is a gem,
So this, my first poem, is just for them!

Damon Inwards (3)
Scribbles Nursery, London

Abigail's First Poem

My name is Abigail and I go to preschool,
My best friend is James, who is really cool.
I watch Peppa Pig on TV,
Playing Barbies and princesses is lots of fun for me.
I just love pasta to eat,
And sometimes cakes for a treat.
Pink is a colour I like a lot,
My princess is the best present I ever got.
My favourite person is Mummy, who is a gem,
So this, my first poem, is just for them!

Abigail Ross (3)
Scribbles Nursery, London

Lyra's First Poem

My name is **Lyra** and I go to preschool,
My best friend is **Jack**, who is really cool.
I watch **The Incredibles** on TV,
Playing **doggy** is lots of fun for me.
I just love **cheesy sweetcorn pasta** to eat,
And sometimes **grapes** for a treat.
Pink is a colour I like a lot,
My **doggy** is the best present I ever got.
My favourite person is **Mummy**, who is a gem,
So this, my first poem, is just for them!

Lyra Price (3)
Scribbles Nursery, London

Saffron's First Poem

My name is Saffron and I go to preschool,
My best friend is Lorna, who is really cool.
I watch Peppa Pig on TV,
Playing dinosaurs is lots of fun for me.
I just love spaghetti to eat,
And sometimes sweets for a treat.
Blue is a colour I like a lot,
My rats are the best present I ever got.
My favourite person is Lorna, who is a gem,
So this, my first poem, is just for them!

Saffron Hardyman (3)
Scribbles Nursery, London

Tuula's First Poem

My name is **Tuula** and I go to preschool,
My best friend is **Jenny**, who is really cool.
I watch **Peter Rabbit** on TV,
Playing **with Roger** is lots of fun for me.
I just love **vegetables** to eat,
And sometimes **chocolate** for a treat.
Purple is a colour I like a lot,
My **mermaid** is the best present I ever got.
My favourite person is **Jenny**, who is a gem,
So this, my first poem, is just for them!

Tuula Price (3)
Scribbles Nursery, London

Isa's First Poem

My name is **Isa** and I go to preschool,
My best friend is **Jack**, who is really cool.
I watch **PAW Patrol** on TV,
Playing **dinosaurs** is lots of fun for me.
I just love **strawberries** to eat,
And sometimes **sweets** for a treat.
Red is a colour I like a lot,
My **Paddington Bear** is the best present I ever got.
My favourite person is **Mummy**, who is a gem,
So this, my first poem, is just for them!

Isa Davis (4)
Scribbles Nursery, London

Ariya's First Poem

My name is **Ariya** and I go to preschool,
My best friend is **Josephine**, who is really cool.
I watch **PAW Patrol** on TV,
Playing **Barbies** is lots of fun for me.
I just love **broccoli** to eat,
And sometimes **cake** for a treat.
Pink is a colour I like a lot,
My **Jasmine quilt** is the best present I ever got.
My favourite person is **Harry**, who is a gem,
So this, my first poem, is just for them!

Ariya Samra (3)
Scribbles Nursery, London

Sammy's First Poem

My name is Sammy and I go to preschool,
My best friend is Mummy, who is really cool.
I watch Andy on TV,
Playing with the ball is lots of fun for me.
I just love pasta to eat,
And sometimes chocolate for a treat.
Blue is a colour I like a lot,
My chocolate is the best present I ever got.
My favourite person is Mummy, who is a gem,
So this, my first poem, is just for them!

Sammy (3)
Scribbles Nursery, London

Henryk's First Poem

My name is Henryk and I go to preschool,
My best friend is Arthur, who is really cool.
I watch dinosaurs on TV,
Playing dinosaurs is lots of fun for me.
I just love macaroni cheese to eat,
And sometimes sweets for a treat.
Red is a colour I like a lot,
My T-rex is the best present I ever got.
My favourite person is Mummy, who is a gem,
So this, my first poem, is just for them!

Henryk Baguet (3)
Scribbles Nursery, London

My First Poem 2017 - North London

Emlyn's First Poem

My name is Emlyn and I go to preschool,
My best friend is Harry, who is really cool.
I watch Peppa Pig on TV,
Playing with fish is lots of fun for me.
I just love fish fingers to eat,
And sometimes sweeties for a treat.
Red is a colour I like a lot,
My taxi is the best present I ever got.
My favourite person is Mummy, who is a gem,
So this, my first poem, is just for them!

Emlyn Moxon (3)
Scribbles Nursery, London

Silver's First Poem

My name is Silver and I go to preschool,
My best friend is Margot, who is really cool.
I watch Peppa Pig on TV,
Playing doctors is lots of fun for me.
I just love chocolate to eat,
And sometimes biscuits for a treat.
Black is a colour I like a lot,
My dolly is the best present I ever got.
My favourite person is Daddy, who is a gem,
So this, my first poem, is just for them!

Silver Emilia Hands Curry (3)
Scribbles Nursery, London

Daniel's First Poem

My name is Daniel and I go to preschool,
My best friend is Saffy, who is really cool.
I watch Peppa on TV,
Playing dinosaurs is lots of fun for me.
I just love spaghetti to eat,
And sometimes a stamp for a treat.
Blue is a colour I like a lot,
My dinosaur is the best present I ever got.
My favourite person is Mummy, who is a gem,
So this, my first poem, is just for them!

Daniel Savigni (3)
Scribbles Nursery, London

Aidan's First Poem

My name is **Aidan** and I go to preschool,
My best friend is **Harry**, who is really cool.
I watch **Spider-Man** on TV,
Playing **with sand** is lots of fun for me.
I just love **chicken** to eat,
And sometimes **chocolate** for a treat.
Red is a colour I like a lot,
My **T-rex** is the best present I ever got.
My favourite person is **Harry**, who is a gem,
So this, my first poem, is just for them!

Aidan Hussain (3)
Scribbles Nursery, London

Jack's First Poem

My name is Jack and I go to preschool,
My best friend is Alice, who is really cool.
I watch Minions on TV,
Playing trucks is lots of fun for me.
I just love pasta to eat,
And sometimes juice for a treat.
Purple is a colour I like a lot,
My dinosaur is the best present I ever got.
My favourite person is Mummy, who is a gem,
So this, my first poem, is just for them!

Jack Cohen (3)
Scribbles Nursery, London

Reyansh's First Poem

My name is **Reyansh** and I go to preschool,
My best friend is **George**, who is really cool.
I watch **PAW Patrol** on TV,
Playing **cars** is lots of fun for me.
I just love **rice** to eat,
And sometimes **cake** for a treat.
Orange is a colour I like a lot,
My **T-rex** is the best present I ever got.
My favourite person is **Mummy**, who is a gem,
So this, my first poem, is just for them!

Reyansh Siaharthan (3)
Scribbles Nursery, London

My First Poem

We hope you have enjoyed reading this book - and that you will continue to enjoy it in the coming years.

If you're a young writer who enjoys reading and creative writing, or the parent of an enthusiastic poet or story writer, do visit our websites, www.myfirstpoem.com and www.youngwriters.co.uk. Here you will find free competitions, workshops and games, as well as recommended reads, a poetry glossary and our blog.

If you would like to order further copies of this book, or any of our other titles, then please give us a call or visit www.myfirstpoem.com.

My First Poem
Remus House
Coltsfoot Drive
Peterborough
PE2 9BF

Tel: 01733 898110
info@myfirstpoem.com